SALLY DUBY

Sales Development Rep Hacks That Work

Step by Step Guide To Success In 59 Days As A SDR In Software & SaaS

This book was professionally typeset on Reedsy.
Find out more at reedsy.com

Contents

1 Introduction   1

2 Month 1: Getting Ready   11

3 Month 2: Test & Refine   28

4 Month 3: Rinse & Repeat   32

About the Author   35

1

Introduction

Sales and Sales Development is a passion of mine and one I've dedicated 37 years to. I got my official start in software sales and sales development in 1986 (I was a teenager at the time- JK) at Oracle. Oracle was a $50M company and when I left 4 years later had just hit the $1B mark. It was quite a ride; I learned a ton. Not just what to do but what not to do.

I started as an inside sales rep working alongside some people that became SaaS visionaries and leaders such as Marc Benioff from Salesforce.com. Marc got his start at Oracle as an inside sales rep and his career obviously skyrocketed. It shows you too can use an inside sales/sales development role on your journey to a huge career in software or SaaS.

At Oracle, I started as a rep and then got promoted to running the Eastern Region of Corporate Sales, then moved to Director of MDRs (Market Development Reps which is known today as Sales Development) and then was Director of Channel Sales. From there I built several teams from scratch and optimized several existing teams. I learned and proved that Sales Development can be equal parts Science and Art (more on that later) and it can be repeatable.

I took that knowledge and worked for 2 different consulting companies specializing in the world of Sales Development and Virtual Sales for B2B (business to business) software and SaaS companies. Over the last 25 years consulting I have talked to and worked with hundreds of different organizations. The SDRs that are successful have mastered the Science and Art of the profession and realize that it's a numbers game of doing enough of the right activities focused on the right companies and buyers within those companies with relevant messaging.

The SDR role remains one of the hardest and most important roles for the Sales team. Without pipeline not much gets sold. It's the hardest job because you endure a lot of no's before you get to that one meeting and a YES! It takes discipline and a lot of routine tasks. The fun and where using your brain comes in is when you get into an active conversation with a prospect uncovering what is top of mind to them and show them how you can help. Then magic happens when you get that meeting set up with an Account Executive (AE).

What's different today from when I first got started?

In some ways in those early days at Oracle, it was simpler. There were only IT and Developer roles most software companies sold to. Most software companies only sold into the technical space and not the end user buyers (like Sales, Marketing, Finance etc.). Knowing who your buyer was and what was important to them was straightforward.

According to AHA there are over 60 different IT roles today and counting. The Data Scientist role is new within the last 10 years, and with the rise of Artificial Intelligence many more new roles have emerged: AI research analyst, AI data engineer, machine language engineer. If you don't even know about these roles, how can you talk to them about what is important to them!

It is much easier for our buyers to do research about us and our products than it was before. They can find out about you and your competitors before you have talked to them. It becomes crucial to talk to them about what is important to them, not about you as the Vendor. I will go into detail about this in the Buyer Persona section. And not only do our buyers have access to lots of information but so do we! We now know exactly who our buyers are by name and role, you should never ask a prospect to tell you who you should talk to!

One area that makes the SDR role easier to do but also adds a layer of complexity is the plethora of sales tools available that are all supposed to make the job easier. At Oracle we didn't have a CRM (Salesforce.com, HubSpot etc.). I'm really going old school here, but I had an index card box that had labels for every month of the year and tabs for 1–31 days of the month. On an index card I wrote down the company and contact name for follow up. I had 3 large binders on my desk where I took hand written notes for every company and contact and date of conversation with next steps. It was one of my happiest days as a rep when we got a CRM!

Today, there are well over 5000 sales tool vendors in the market (if you are interested in seeing the landscape of sales tools- check them out here https://tenbound.com/directory/?lid=3 137). We are over saturated now in tools and too many tools can actually slow you down and impede your success. More technology is not necessarily better. There are a handful of categories of tools that are table stakes now that you need to have. Keep in mind, if your process is bad or your messaging is bad, automating it with a tool keeps it bad, you are just sending out a lot more crap.

For New SDRs and SDRs in the role today wanting to improve.

This book is intended to help both new and current SDRs who are continually looking to become the top SDR. One of the challenges in software and SaaS companies today is that we haven't done a good job of training SDR and Sales Leaders in how to set up SDRs for success. I talk to these companies every day, so trust me in this!You will encounter a situation where you get hired, trained on the product and then are told you go figure it out. You may be that 1 in 500 SDR that through perseverance, lots of trial and error, and frustration finally finds success. Or you can follow a proven process to be successful quickly, meet quota and get your promotion. The choice is yours.

I'm going to share a story of a company I worked with as a Fractional Sales Leader. The company was at an early stage in their SaaS Journey. They had about 8 SDRs and 14 Sales Reps. Everyone was doing something different. There were no standards, no specific messaging in place, no guidelines in activities and goals. They had sales tools that they used for 1 month and forgot about. Very few SDRs and Sales Reps were making quota, yet they continued to hire more people. The changes I made were all the ones I'm going to go into detail in the rest of the book. They were going after a segment of the market that didn't renew their contracts and wouldn't sign year contracts. It wasn't profitable for the business.

Once we understood the Ideal Customer Profile and Buyers within the company, I figured out what the individual SDR quota should be that was realistic and provided the number of meetings the sales team needed to make their quota.

From there I could figure out the number of activities and type of activities SDRs needed to do daily, weekly, and monthly to hit their goal of setting up meetings. I had them focus on the top 3 buyer persona roles, gave them the complete sequence, with the touch points, how often and what each exact message should be. And made sure they had access to the data needed to figure out who to add to their list. I had written up a talk track for the call opening if someone actually answered the phone to ensure the SDRs were comfortable making phone calls. Then we trained, practiced, and coached on all this information.

The results: less chaos, SDRs had daily action plans, activities increased 2.5 times which resulted in double the meetings setting (with the right companies) and the SDRs made quota which allowed more AEs to meet quota. I was able to promote 50% of the SDRs into AE roles.

Understanding Terms

Here's some common terms you will hear thrown around. Most of these are standard terms but sometimes companies put their own spin on them so clarify if you are starting with a new company what their meaning is, so you are on the same page (especially for the top 3 terms below).

MQL- Marketing Qualified Lead

An MQL is a lead that Marketing generated from Ads, Webinars, Podcasts, website, forms filled in on website, events etc. MQL- SQL and SAL are terms coined by Sirius Decisions (part of Forrester Research group).

Marketing rates the lead on actions or actions they take and hopefully include in the rating if the lead is within the Ideal Customer Profile and Buyer Persona. Only leads with certain scores then get passed to the SDRs to follow up with, establish need and interest in talking further and then setting a meeting. Inbound leads are considered Warm vs Cold leads and typically easier to work than Outbound Cold leads.

SQL- Sales Qualified Lead

Sales Rep (AE) has formally accepted this prospect from the SDR after their initial scheduled call set by the SDR. The prospect meets the criteria established and the prospect is willing to have another conversation and move to the next stage in the sales cycle.

SAL- Sales Accepted Lead

This can be removed as a Step or even added before the SQL step. It essentially says that marketing sends a lead and Sales or SDRs decide whether it meets initial criteria for them to work on- is it from the Ideal Customer Profile and the right buyer persona.

Inbound Lead

Is basically an MQL and the prospect proactively reaching out to the company. The contact knows who you are, and this is considered a WARM lead and easier to follow up with than a cold call. Not all inbound leads are created equal. A person that fills out a request for a demo on your website is a way better lead than someone who downloads a white paper from your website.

Outbound or Cold Call

Unsolicited contact attempt to a prospect because your company has determined their company, and their role/title are a good fit for your product or service. It takes more outbound contacts to convert to a meeting.

Account Based Marketing/Sales/Everything (ABM, ABS or ABE)

Could also be known as Strategic or Target Account sales.

This is typically reserved for a smaller number of high-profile accounts that your company has determined they really want as a customer because they are well-known names and would be very large deals. The account list is typically determined by sales and marketing leaders. Then the specific roles/titles/contacts are added. Because these are large accounts- there could be 50-150 names for each account. Who follows up could be segmented by title or role, for example the AE may go after the VP level roles, SDRs may be assigned the Director or Manager level roles and VPs may even be assigned the C level roles. The messaging and call to action (CTA) may be focused on an event coming up. The messaging should be highly customized for each contact.

Lead Process

This is the process that a lead (MQL or Outbound) goes through to become a prospect and moves to Sales. Typically, it contains the following:

- New
- Attempting to reach
- Contacted/not contacted/qualified or disqualified
- Meeting set,
- Meeting held then SQL.
- Didn't reach, Nurture

Sales Cycle/Process

This is the process the AE goes through once you set up a meeting to eventually/hopefully close a deal. There are typically anywhere from 4 to 10 steps in the sales process depending on the complexity of the product and the price. The more complex the product and the higher the price point (think like $100,000+) the more steps to close it.

Typical steps are:

- Qualify
- Validate
- Demo/Trial
- Propose
- Negotiate
- Close

Buyers Journey

The buyers journey came about in the last 15 years. It is acknowledging that our buyers have different processes they go through to buy software than what our sales process is. So, you need to overlap the sales process with their buying journey to ensure we are taking care of what our buyers are looking to accomplish at each engagement phase. Typical steps in buyers journey:

- Develop business plan
- Understand the impact to the business
- Determine requirements & budget
- Evaluate options
- Shortlist solutions/vendors
- Negotiate
- Close

Conversions

Conversions are the results of the activities. For example, if an SDR talks to 10 people and 2 of them agree to meet with an AE that is a 20% conversion rate. Another example: an SDR sets up 10 meetings for AEs and 9 of those meetings take place, that is a 90% conversion rate. This is a way to compare against industry best practices, other SDRs on your team and set goals and objectives.

Sequence/Cadence

Sequence and or Cadence refers to the number of touch points, the type of touch and the message you use when you are following up on an MQL or doing outbound cold calling.

A typical outbound sequence will have 10-12 steps over a 20−25-day period of time.

- Touch 1 may start with a phone call (leave a message if no answer,
- Touch 2 would be 2 days later with a LinkedIn connection

request,

● Touch 3 would be 3 days later with an email with specific messaging

And so on.

There is a category of software SDRs use to execute this easily called Sales Engagement Platforms. Outreach, SalesLoft, Salesvue, Apollo, Revenue Grid are all examples of this software.

2

Month 1: Getting Ready

If you are new to a company or this is your first SDR role, most software companies are great at providing lots of product training. Product training is always helpful but there is so much more than just product training for you to do your job properly and see success. Many software companies lack in providing you the information you need to do your job successfully. In this chapter, I will discuss what other information you need and ways to go about getting it if you haven't received this information from your manager, training classes or marketing.

For current SDRs, if you never got this information during your training, start getting it now or validate what you think you know. No matter how long you have been at the company, following these steps can help you improve your results.

Learn from the top SDRs and AEs in your company

Seek out the top SDRs and AEs. Ask if you can pick their brains and learn from them.

Here's some questions to ask them:

For AEs:

- Why are they doing that makes them the top AE?
- Do they have a different process from others? Different message?
- How does the AE work with their SDR?
- What does the AE expect from their SDR?

For SDRs:

- How many activities/day does the SDR do?
- What type of activities do they do- more email, more phone, more LinkedIn?
- What companies are they targeting?
- What buyer persona's?
- What messaging are they using?
- What do they suggest you do to be as successful as they are?
- What makes them the top SDR? What are they doing differently than the other SDRs?

If you can listen to any recorded calls from the top SDR so you can hear how they do the call opening, what questions they ask, how the prospect responds to them is extremely helpful for you.

Understand your Ideal Customer Profile

What companies are you targeting? This can be defined by employee size, revenue size, a vertical such as the type of industry- manufacturing companies or finance companies, or insurance companies, education etc. Ask questions about where the sweet spot is, where do you find the most success. You want to focus and narrow your target company list as much as possible.

If you are told to go after companies that are over 1000 employees, according to Statistia there are over 8300 companies and NAICS says there are over 24,000 companies in the US that meet that criteria. You are one person; you will never get to those companies in your time as an SDR. An SDR can contact roughly 150-225 accounts per month (depending on how many contacts per account and the number of steps in the sequence. You can see how long it would take you to get to all those accounts. Finding ones that have a problem you can solve and are willing to talk further is comparable to finding a needle in a haystack. You want to understand your "sweet spot" or best chance of success.Further detail on the ideal customer profile company besides size, to narrow the list down to something more manageable- like a vertical or a company that is being acquired that has over 1000 employees. These are the companies you want to focus on first.

You can talk to Marketing, Product Marketing, Sales Enablement, Sales Operations, Sales Leaders as well as the top AEs and SDRs about this.

Understand your Buyer Persona's

Once you have your focused list of accounts you are going to call, who within the account are you going after specifically? What is the role or title of the persona you want to reach and get a meeting set with. This is the person that has the problems you solve and has the capability to decide to buy your product. It could be the VP of IT, it could be VP of Finance, or Director of

DevOps. There are most likely multiple roles you want to reach out to within one company.

You want to understand a little bit about the role, their responsibilities and what the typical challenges are. An easy way to understand this is to use AI - ChatGPT. As of now the free version works just fine. It can tell you in seconds. Your prompt can be something like:

I'm selling to (job title). Please tell me what their primary top 3 responsibilities are and their top 5 business challenges and what is the business effect if they don't do anything about that challenge.

Once you have the challenges by buyer persona you need to understand the business value you provide. This means you will probably need help from product marketing or marketing.

Understanding what is important to your buyer is critical. This is how you want to approach them in your messaging. It's all about the buyer not about you, the vendor! Remember that! You can try ChatGPT again with a prompt:

I'm selling a (your solution description) to (this type of company), and (buyer persona). Can you deep dive into what their pain points might be and how my solution can solve their challenges.

An example of this prompt would look like-
I'm selling a budget and forecasting solution to the VP of Finance in enterprise prospects in the manufacturing industry. Can you deep dive into what the VP of Finance pain points might be and how my solutions can solve their challenges?

With any AI response please validate the information and edit it before sending it or using it. It can be a good starting point but too raw to send to any prospects as is.

Here's a sample Buyer Persona for a Marketing Operations or CRM Manager:

Responsibilities:

Ultimate responsibility for creating and executing email marketing campaigns that maximize revenue opportunities from the landscape of "known customers".

● Segment the customer database in order to deliver personalized messages to the right customer at the right time.

● Manage the company's outbound campaigns and communicate the company brand and key offers through email marketing.

● Analyze the success of email marketing campaigns and make recommendations for improvement.

● Ensure all email campaigns comply with current email best practices.

● Measure revenue derived from email campaigns.

● Break down silos in order to integrate disparate customer data and gain a 360 degree of the customer.

Challenges:

● Plummeting engagement

● Opens, click-throughs, time on site, conversions, etc.

● Rising unsubscribes

● Being pressured to increase conversions

● Inability to access all the information needed (i.e. psychographic data) to drive effective segmentation

In the section about Writing your Sequences you will see how you use this information in detail.

Do more research

Understanding your buyers and the value you bring to those buyers is the most important aspect of the job you can learn. Besides the top sales reps, SDRs, Sales and Marketing Leaders, we discussed above you can talk to your internal Customer Success reps (CSMs), Customer Support or Account Managers. These are the people that typically work with existing customers, not new customers.

- Ask them about customer success stories.
  - What was the role/title of the actual buyer
  - What problem were they trying to solve when they bought your product
  - What results have they achieved with your product
  - Are there additional results they got they weren't expecting

Read your marketing materials on customer stories. These are great stories to learn so you can share them as examples in conversations with prospects. They should give you more information on the value you provide.

One of my favorite people to talk to within your own company, is the title of the person you are prospecting to. If your buyer persona is the VP of Finance- talk to the VP of Finance at your company. Or if your buyer persona is the CIO- Chief Information Officer if your company has a CIO or equivalent role ask for a meeting. *Ask them:*
- What are your key responsibilities

● What are your top 3-5 business challenges

● Are they using your product and what are the biggest benefits they get from using it

● What would catch their eye and cause them to respond to a call or email from you?

● Do they have a preferred method of communication (LinkedIn, email, Phone, Video)

Understand The Math Of Meeting Quota

Most companies will give an SDR a quota based on the number of meetings set per month. Some may add other components such as the number of meetings that take place and they AE determines there is enough need an interest to move to the next step in the sales cycle - SQL.

It's awesome that you know what you need to produce to meet quota and make a bonus or commission. What effort and activities will it take to get to 15 meetings per month? That's where many organizations fail their SDRs. They don't give you guidelines to follow to help you get to your quota. Too many managers like to say they only manage outcomes (meaning quota numbers). What happens when you don't meet quota? How do you know what to change, or do differently to meet quota? As a leader I prefer to set my reps up for success and show them the path up front, so they have all the tools, techniques, and content to be successful right away.

Sales and Sales Development is both art and science. The art is being able to have conversations, show you understand your prospect and how you can bring value. Building a credible relationship with the prospect is mostly art. The science is the process and messaging to follow to engage a prospect to set a meeting, to move forward with the next steps in the sales cycle. The science is also understanding that 100% of people in your sales pipeline will NOT buy! 100% of the people you reach in prospecting WON'T respond, 100% of the people you talk to WON'T agree to set up a meeting. In my 35+ years in sales and Sales Development, I have never seen near a 100% close rate in anything. Which is why this is a game of numbers. Much like betting, you don't win every bet you make, you only win a portion of them or there would be no one willing to take bets if they knew they would always lose.

The number of activities you need to do daily, weekly, and monthly is critical to your success.

Here's some numbers to keep in mind. They come from the consulting company, The Bridge Group, I work for. We are known for our SDR Benchmark Report.

If you aren't being set up for success, follow the path outlined below.

- SDRs need to do on average 104 activities every day of every month to generate 14 meetings per month.
- Approximately 40 emails, 40 calls, 16 linked in, 2 text and 6 in the other category.
- If you make 40 calls/day you will talk to about 9–10% (conversion) of those or 3.6 quality conversations per day (meaning you reached the right person and got some information).
- Of the 40 emails you send per day you will only get a 1–2% response rate (conversion) or less than 1 per day!

Understanding LinkedIn conversions is more difficult to track the results because not many systems are integrated to LinkedIn. It's up to you as the SDR to mark the attempt as a LinkedIn out-reach but more importantly if someone responds via LinkedIn you have to mark the response as from LinkedIn in your CRM.

Let's say you connect with 5 people per day, typically 10-15% of those you have a conversation with will convert to a meeting set. On the high end that means you will set less than one meeting per day or slightly less than 4 per week (3.75 per week). Over the course of a month that would be 15 meetings set.

● These numbers will vary based on the type of outreach you are doing- inbound or outbound, the segment of accounts you go after (enterprise, mid-market, or SMB) and the average deal size. Outbound only, the numbers will go down slightly.
   ● Calling large enterprises with the typical average deal size of $500,000 you may only set 3-5 meetings per month.
   ● Inbound lead conversions will be higher, and you could set 30-40 meetings per month.

Let's assume you are doing mostly outbound prospecting to enterprise prospects with an average deal size of $100,000. Here's what the numbers look like:

	Per SDR		
	day	month	year
Estimated Call/Email attempts	100	2000	24,000
# Connects	5.0	100	960
Connect converts to Meeting	1	15	144
Meeting Pipeline	75,000	1,500,000	14,400,000
Meeting converts to next stage	0.4	8	72
AE Pipeline	$37,500	$750,000	$7,200,000

This paints the picture that based on standard SDR conversions you need to consistently do a lot of activities every day to make your numbers.

If you are new, use this as a baseline. After 3 months you can start plugging in your numbers and conversions and see how it changes your needed activity levels and results.

If you are currently an SDR plug in your own numbers, conversions to help you devise a new game plan to help you increase your results. Hopefully you have access to dashboards and reports that can give you this data. If not, ask your manager or Sales Operations for these numbers. You should also be able to see what the top performing SDRs are doing on their numbers so you can work to replicate what they are doing.

Without this information, it's like a pilot flying blind!

Write Your Sequences by Buyer Persona

We know how many activities per day we need, but where are those activities coming from? They will come from your Sequences by Buyer Persona that dictate how many steps, what kind of outreach you will do (email, phone, LinkedIn) on what day along with the message for each step.

This is where the research you did earlier comes into play. Your message will be based on the different challenges/pain points for that buyer persona.

Number of Steps

According to The Bridge Group SDR Benchmark Report referenced earlier, the average number of steps for an outbound sequence today is 11. So, let's start with an 11-step sequence.

Multi-Media Approach

This refers to the different types of outreach you are going to do, email, phone, text, video, LinkedIn, Instagram, Facebook. Every person has preferred communication methods and different roles find certain ways of communicating with them preferable. For instance, very few C level roles in the Fortune 500 companies will have LinkedIn profiles, many CFO's, VPs of Finance are not big on LinkedIn communication either. You want to map your outreach attempts to what seems to be their preferred method of communication. If you don't know, start with the big 3- email, phone, and LinkedIn. Later, you can test video, texting etc.

Messaging Themes by Buyer Persona

This is the most important step, the messaging! You can reach out the appropriate number of times with a variety of different methods but if your message is wrong your prospect still won't respond to you. Remember this important point, especially in outbound prospecting, your prospect does NOT care about your company at this point.They don't care how large you are, or that you are the "best" or that an industry analyst put you in the magic quadrant or that XYZ company is a client. All your prospect cares about at this point is can you help them solve a big problem they have been dealing with and make their life easier! That's it. Giving a customer story at this point is useless. Once you have them engaged in an actual conversation referencing a short customer story as a proof point is appropriate and useful but not until you are engaged in a conversation.

Your prospect wants you to show them that you understand them and can help them. They don't want "cutesy" or funny messages. Anyone at a VP level or C level won't be swayed by offering them cupcakes or an Amazon or Starbucks gift card to take a meeting. As a matter of fact, they will be insulted more than anything.

We want to create a different theme for each touch-point and medium you are using. If we go back to our Marketing Operations/ CRM Manager buyer persona example here's a sample of creating themes by touch point:

Touch 1 VM: Open rates, click through
    Touch 2 LI: Connection request- brand communication
    Touch 3 EM: Personalization
    Touch 4 VM: Measuring revenue from campaigns
    Touch 5 Call No VM: Customer lifetime value
    Touch 6 EM: Rising unsubscribes

Touch 7 VM: Communicating across digital touch-points
Touch 8 EM: Increase conversions
Touch 9 Final VM
Touch 10 Final EM
Touch 11 LinkedIn InMail

Every touch point is spaced 2-3 days apart from each other.

As you see we used the responsibilities and challenges for the role to create the themes.

Every touch is a different message. We don't just keep hitting them over the head addressing the same challenge repeatedly. We want to give them as many different reasons to want to talk with us as possible. One of those over time is likely to resonate with them.

Now that we know what each message will be about, we want to create the actual message for each touch point. This way you don't have to stop and think about what to say, it's already done and you can be more efficient and productive and get to your 100+ activities each day.

And if you are saying the same thing to the same buyer persona at each step of the way when you look at where the responses are coming from you know what message is working and which ones to tweak. This will get you to a repeatable scalable prospecting process- Rinse and Repeat.

Voicemail Best Practices:
- Less than 40 seconds
- Avoid mentioning product names or features

- Use language and terminology important to them
- Don't use your product jargon
- Practice your VM out loud.
- Does it sound natural and clear
- Is it about your buyer not you

Email Best Practices

- No more than 3 paragraphs that are no more than 2-3 sentences each.
- Not too formal but not informal- no Hey Dudes!
- Use Data or proof points or reports from 3rd parties or your company that correlate to the theme
- Call to action: ask them if they would like to learn more
- Read it aloud- does it flow and sound natural

Using our Buyer Persona example of Marketing Operations, here's sample messages that correspond to our themes above:

Touch 1 VM- Open rates & click throughs

Hi (name). I've heard from many Marketing operations managers that when it comes to lowering unsubscribe rates, providing personalized and targeted emails are key. Would you like to learn more about leveraging unified customer data to boost email open rates and click-throughs? You can text me at xxx-xxxx. This is (your name) from xyz company

Touch 2 LinkedIn Message with connection request on brand communication

First name,

Are you having trouble rising above the digital noise? Would leveraging demographic, psychographic, and behavioral data help you facilitate one to one brand communication?

Would you be open to learning more?

Your name

Outbound Call Openings

This is another important area you need to be ready for. When you make a call, you want your prospect to answer your call. Then what happens! You have to be ready to Go!

I have found it is much easier to be prepared when you have a talk track written out and easily accessible. Write out your talk track, practice and keep practicing until it feels comfortable to you.

Here is an outbound call opening I like and works well for me when I call VPs of Sales:

Hi (name). I know you weren't expecting my call. And yes, this is a cold call. But if you have about 27 seconds, I can tell you why I'm calling and then you can tell me if you'd like to keep chatting. By the way, this is Sally Duby from The Bridge Group.

Thanks. I talk to a lot of VPs of Sales, and they tell me they are focused on one of two things:

1- increasing pipeline

2- decreasing sales cycle length.

Which one of those is a bigger focus for you now?

Now they will tell me which one or tell me neither of those are - this is what my focus is now. Then I can pivot and talk more about that issue and ask if they are open to scheduling time to talk more.

You can see I continue to use buyer persona messaging and challenges associated with that buyer. It's about them not about me and my company!

Any skeptics out there if this will really work? Don't believe me. Ok, story time. At The Bridge Group (www.bridgegroupinc.com)

we worked with a mid-size SaaS company that had 65 SDRs. They were doing both inbound and outbound. The company wanted to move to more enterprise accounts and get larger deal sizes. They knew they would need to do a lot more outbound prospecting to get to those enterprise accounts. They took 50 of the 65 SDRs and made them outbound only. They figured since they had been doing outbound, they didn't need much in the way of training and support. Well, after 6 months of this change the combined 50 SDRs had $0 in the pipeline!

Not surprisingly, the sales and marketing leaders were freaking out. The Bridge Group was hired to help fix this because of our reputation, knowledge, and expertise in the SDR world.

We did a whole ton of different things, but the biggest improvement came when we developed a Playbook for the SDRs based on Buyer Persona messaging sequences (explained above) and trained the SDRs. According to our client, at the **end of two months** after training here's what happened:

→Activities increased 7X

→Meetings scheduled also increased 7X

→Each SDR was averaging $500,000 in pipeline generated from the meetings (up from $0!)

Hopefully you are a believer and are willing to do the work and put in the effort outlined!

Data Preparation

Once you have your messages developed, and edited, you are ready to put them into your sales engagement platform (think Outreach, Salesloft, Salesvue etc.). Once they are in there you can start assigning contacts to the appropriate Buyer Persona sequence. Every day you will be guided to what tasks are due and what the messaging is.

Word of caution- don't go crazy assigning more than 8

contacts per day to a Sequence. Or by the following week you will have way too many tasks due daily that you won't be able to complete them. This is when we see bad behavior begin, you end up skipping steps or not completing a contact all the way through the 11-step sequence. Which lowers your chances of reaching the number of prospects you need to make your number.

You want to make sure you are dispositioning each activity.

- Left a Voice message,
- Sent Linked in
- Sent email
- Ghost call- called, no answer and didn't leave a voicemail
- Connected- Set meeting for AE (prospect answered phone)
- Connected- couldn't talk asked to call back
- Connected- no need
- What other options could there be?

3

Month 2: Test & Refine

Go Time

You spent the time preparing and getting set up, now it's go time to execute your plan.

1. Follow your sequences by buyer persona.
2. Complete your tasks every day.
3. Assign contacts to the appropriate sequences so you can get to 100 activities daily.
4. Start getting a feel for what is resonating with people when you talk to them, or they respond to emails or LinkedIn.
5. Block out time on your calendar every day to do your calls and don't do anything else until the calls are complete.
6. Monitor your activities daily and weekly.
7. What are your conversions– how many people are responding by email, call, LinkedIn?
8. How many connects to a meeting set?

If you are an SDR looking to improve your results, how are they looking compared to your previous results- better, worse, or the same? Why?

Don't get caught up in vanity metrics- metrics around emails that can make you feel good but don't lead to the end result you need - typically things like open email rates and positive response rates tracked by your sales engagement platform. If you have high open rates and positive response rates but you aren't engaged and getting meetings set- it doesn't matter how high your open rates are. Always remember your job is to get a meeting set with the right company and the right buyer persona!

Refine

Before you make any changes, you must have enough data to tell you what is working and isn't working. One day's worth of data isn't enough. Typically, you need a good 4 weeks of actively doing 100 activities/days and working prospects through a complete sequence of 11 steps before you can make appropriate judgments. This is an area where you probably need the advice of your manager or director or even sales operations to help you figure out where there are steps in your sequence that are working and aren't working.

If your connection rate making calls is only 3-4% it most often is because you have bad phone numbers, calling general office phone numbers not direct dial phone numbers. Or if you're calling companies and personas that are more often working remotely, you need access to accurate mobile numbers! Pre-

Covid, calling mobile numbers was not something we did, but since Covid calling mobile numbers is the best way to reach your prospects and is acceptable. There is one product that stands far above all the others for providing the greatest number of accurate mobile numbers, Modigie www.modigie.com.Tell them I told you to call!

A-B testing is a great way to test different messages or parts of messages to see which performs better. But it can get complicated doing A-B testing right. And you can't change everything in the message. It's best to talk to marketing operations, or sales operations about how to do an A- B test.

If you would like objective feedback on your messaging, ask your AE or manager about it. Or if you have the buyer persona role in your company, ask them how they feel about the messages you have. Or send me a few of your messages with who the buyer persona is and I'm happy to provide you with feedback. Send it to sduby@bridgegroupinc.com with a subject title of **please review my messages**. I have offered this to hundreds of SDR Leaders and so far, only 1 has taken me up on the offer.

Hand-off to AE

Once you have an agreement from a prospect to meet with your AE you must set up the meeting on your prospect and AEs calendar. Hopefully you have access to your AEs calendar, so you know when they are available. Here's some best practices to follow that will help increase the % of prospects that show up for the scheduled meeting. If you have less than 90% show rate for meetings scheduled you need to improve your process, or your buyer persona focus.

● Schedule calls within 5 days or no more than 10 days out unless they are on vacation during that time.

● Send the calendar invite out ASAP.

● Email them if they haven't accepted the calendar invite after 48 hours.

● Send a reminder email or text, this is a great use of texting, within 2 hours of the scheduled meeting.

● Ensure your AE has access to your notes from the call and what the prospect is interested in.

4

Month 3: Rinse & Repeat

If doesn't matter if you are a first time SDR or new to a company but have been an SDR before, typical ramp up time (the time it takes you to get up to hitting your full quota month after month) is 3 months. Right now, you should be seeing good results and, on your way to hitting your quota.

Keep tracking your results and learn what your unique conversions are and what is working for you.

If you are struggling at any stage, ask for help! Don't be afraid. Ask your manager, or the top SDR for advice. Or get ideas from peers outside of your company that you trust.

The last thing I want to address is setting realistic expectations for promotions. The Bridge Group did a study on SDR promotions to the AE role several years ago,

Here's what we learned:
The post-promotion failure rate for SDRs to an AE with 11

or fewer months experience was 55% at one company.

The failure rate for SDRs to an AE with 16+ months experience was just 6%.

The morale of the story is patience. If you push it to happen too fast, you are most likely setting yourself up for failure as an AE. Learn everything you can while in the role. Hopefully, your company offers a great SDR career progression path, that allows you promotions within the SDR role and access to additional training and resources that will prepare you even more for the AE role if that's what you want. For instance, once you reach a Sr. SDR role, you get access to an AE to "ride along" with them 2 days/month to sit with them and learn what they do, or maybe you get access to sales enablement to work with you on how to give a demo or do a discovery call. These kinds of training that you don't get to do as an SDR will better prepare you for success as an AE. If your company doesn't offer this, ASK for training!

We know that being an AE is not for everyone. The good news is there are plenty of SDR opportunities for promotions that aren't sales related. I have seen an increase in SDRs moving to the following roles over the last 5 years or so:
- SDR Manager or Team Lead
- Operations
- Enablement
- Marketing
- Content writing- writing SDR messaging
- Account Management/Customer Success

You have lots of options ahead of you, after you prove yourself as an SDR.

Go show 'em what you got!

If you found this book helpful, I'd be appreciative if you left a positive review for the book on Amazon.

About the Author

Sally is passionate about Virtual Sales and Sales Development and helping others learn how to build world-class virtual sales organizations that are repeatable and scalable. Sally has been an industry speaker at various Sales Conferences, Webinars and VC firms. She is co- founder and board member of the VP of Sales Forum in the Bay Area former AA-ISP Silicon Valley Chapter Board Member and was named one of the Top 25 Most Influential Inside Sales Executives, a Forbes Business Council member and a published Forbes writer.

Sally is CSO and Partner at The Bridge Group, Inc, today's most respected and influential inside sales and sales development consultancy working with tech stars such as Coupa Software, Avalara, Bill.com, Dropbox , to IBM, CA, Oracle and Autodesk. She is also an advisor to many companies such as WindRiver, Streamsend, Imperva, Galvanize and others.

Previously, she was Interim VP of Sales for a SaaS start up, head of sales for Skype, and ran another inside sales consultancy for 15 years. Sally learned all about inside sales starting as an inside sales rep and working her way up to leadership roles at Oracle in the late 80s and then built and ran inside sales teams at Network General and Ingres.

You can connect with me on:

- https://www.bridgegroupinc.com
- https://www.linkedin.com/in/sallyduby